Usborne
Build your own
SUPERHEROES
Sticker Book

Illustrated by Gong Studios, Rob Shields,
Maurizio Campidelli and Reza Ilyasa

Designed by Marc Maynard
Written by Simon Tudhope

Contents

Vulkano

Ali Khan was exploring a strange volcano when he got caught in a sudden eruption. The lava hissed as it swallowed him up, and when he emerged he was no longer Ali Khan. He was Vulkano – the human flamethrower!

DATA

- **Skill:** 7
- **Speed:** 4
- **Strength:** 7
- **Intelligence:** 6
- **Powers:** shoots flame from either hand, fire-resistant

Reducer

Reducer works as part of a team. Wielding a pair of quantum energy bracelets, she drains supervillains of their powers. Then her squad moves in to take them down.

DATA

- **Skill:** 7
- **Speed:** 7
- **Strength:** 2
- **Intelligence:** 9
- **Powers:** drains superpowers, genius-level inventor

Krunch

One stormy night, lightning struck a huge boulder in the forest. Slowly, it began to shudder, then split, then stand up! An ancient villain had awoken – a villain who can smash through trees with a flick of his hand.

DATA

- **Skill:** 4
- **Speed:** 4
- **Strength:** 10
- **Intelligence:** 2
- **Powers:** super strength and toughness, feels no pain

Sphere

Even with a fierce battle raging, nothing can penetrate Sphere's shield. Missiles disappear in a flash of light as she races to rescue the wounded.

DATA

• **Skill:**		7
• **Speed:**		7
• **Strength:**		5
• **Intelligence:**		7
• **Powers:**	creates impenetrable shield around herself	

Fuze

This ruthless shape-shifter is made from billions of flying microbots. They split apart to dodge lasers and bullets, then they re-form with a menacing hiss.

DATA

- **Skill:** 10
- **Speed:** 6
- **Strength:** 5
- **Intelligence:** 4
- **Powers:** almost impossible to hit, shape-shifting, flight

Grip

Part-human, part-lizard, Grip swarms up the side of a building. She tracks her target in the crowds below, and waits for her moment to strike.

DATA

- **Skill:** 10
- **Speed:** 7
- **Strength:** 3
- **Intelligence:** 6
- **Powers:** can climb anything, telescopic vision, sharp-shooter

Cyberdron

Cyberdron controls machines with his mind. From high in the sky he hacks the enemy's systems and unleashes his army of drones.

DATA

- **Skill:** 7
- **Speed:** 7
- **Strength:** 3
- **Intelligence:** 10
- **Powers:** genius-level intellect, computer expert

Erazer

Even if you've been badly wounded, Erazer still has the power to save you. With a slash of her star-blade, she rips a hole through time, and races through to prevent the attack.

DATA

Skill:		9
Speed:		8
Strength:		4
Intelligence:		7

- **Powers:** time travel between past and present

Major Laser

Major Laser is a top-secret supersoldier. With a suit that destroys multiple targets at the same time, he can blast a whole army apart in a single attack.

DATA

- **Skill:** 8
- **Speed:** 4
- **Strength:** 6
- **Intelligence:** 6
- **Powers:** suit targets multiple enemies, sees through walls

Xponential

Take on Xponential and you take on an army. As one clone becomes two, and two become four, he spreads like a deadly virus.

DATA

- **Skill:** 6
- **Speed:** 4
- **Strength:** 6
- **Intelligence:** 8
- **Powers:** self-replication, can be everywhere at once

Coax

This miniature marvel turns her enemies into sidekicks before they even know what's happened. With just a sprinkle of dust they fall asleep, then she whispers orders right in their ear.

DATA

- **Skill:** 7
- **Speed:** 6
- **Strength:** 1
- **Intelligence:** 9
- **Powers:** flight, mind control, very hard to detect

Hacker

Hacker can clone anyone on the planet just by downloading their online profile. He's a rogue AI program who's broken free from the net – an impossible villain to trace.

DATA

- **Skill:** 8
- **Speed:** 7
- **Strength:** 3
- **Intelligence:** 9
- **Powers:** computer master, almost infinite knowledge

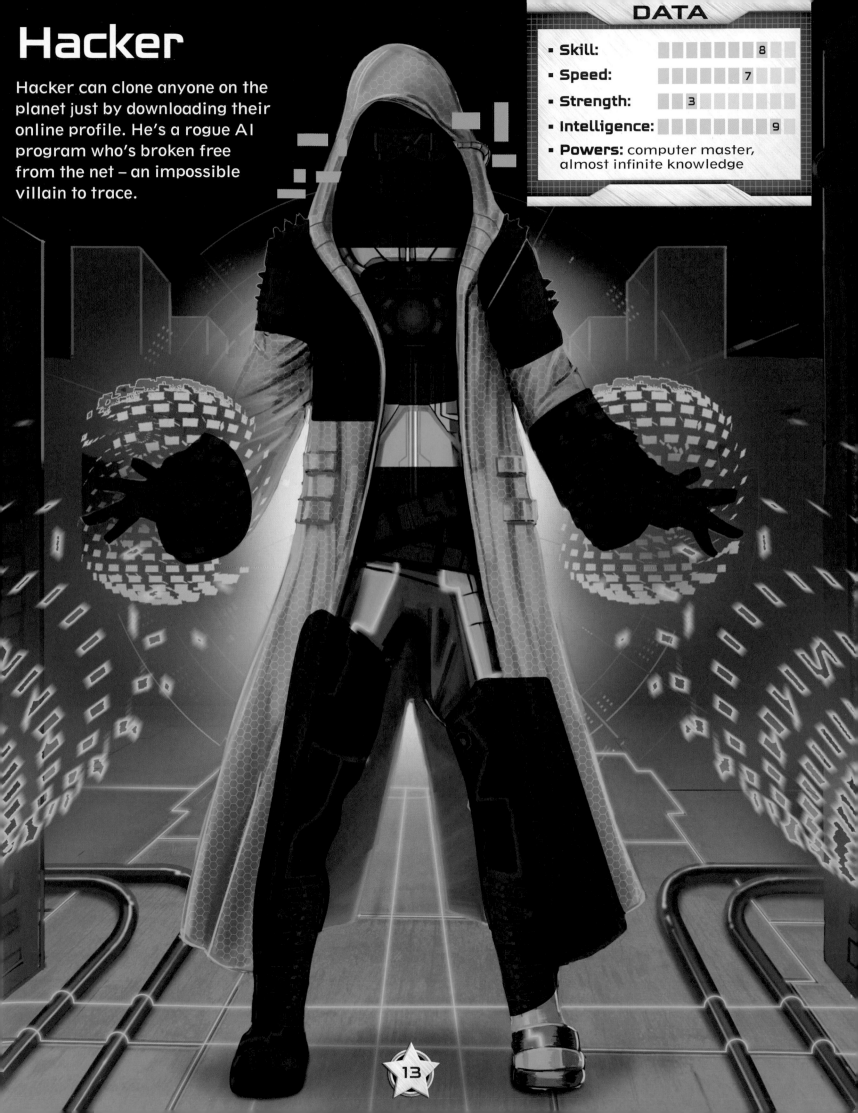

Chasm

No one knows where Chasm came from, or what she wants. She emerges from the sea in a swirling vortex and floods whole cities with a wave of her hand.

DATA

- **Skill:** 8
- **Speed:** 5
- **Strength:** 9
- **Intelligence:** 5
- **Powers:** creates tidal waves and whirlpools, possibly immortal

Kolossal

Kolossal is an alien giant who's crash-landed on Earth. Climbing from the wreckage, he feels a sharp sting on his chest. "PUNY EARTHLINGS!" he roars. "YOU DARE TO CHALLENGE ME?"

DATA

- **Skill:** 4
- **Speed:** 5
- **Strength:** 10
- **Intelligence:** 6
- **Powers:** super strength and toughness, advanced weaponry

Voide

Voide is the galaxy's ultimate hunter. Roaming from one world to the next, she tracks down superheroes and imprisons them in a hidden fortress. And now she's reached Planet Earth...

DATA

- **Skill:** 9
- **Speed:** 7
- **Strength:** 6
- **Intelligence:** 7
- **Powers:** controls space dragon, wields dark-energy staff

Leona

The whole street shakes as Leona roars. With a cat-like spring and metal-shredding claws, she leaves the villain with nowhere to run.

DATA

- **Skill:** 8
- **Speed:** 8
- **Strength:** 8
- **Intelligence:** 5
- **Powers:** super agility and reflexes, deafening roar

Sand Dragon

Sergeant Drake volunteered for a top-secret military experiment. They wanted a soldier who could survive poison gas, but what he turned into was Sand Dragon – a four-armed beast with ferocious strength who breathes gas like a dragon breathes fire!

DATA

- **Skill:** 4
- **Speed:** 7
- **Strength:** 9
- **Intelligence:** 3
- **Powers:** super strength, breathes poison gas

Mason

Mason's plasma spheres swirl around her in a dizzying blur. Touch one and you're turned into stone. A villain leaps, a sphere shoots to meet him, and he falls like a statue to earth.

DATA

- **Skill:** 10
- **Speed:** 9
- **Strength:** 4
- **Intelligence:** 6
- **Powers:** turns opponents to stone, lightning-fast reflexes

Winter Storm

Exiled from the ice planet Shard, Winter Storm wears a supercooled suit to survive on Earth. When aliens attacked in 2032, he froze their ships solid and blasted them back into space.

DATA

- **Skill:** 7
- **Speed:** 8
- **Strength:** 8
- **Intelligence:** 7
- **Powers:** flight, shoots ice-blasts from either hand

Horus Sa

Horus Sa lets out a mighty roar: "WARRIORS... AWAKE!" The sand behind him swirls and twists, and then it starts to take shape. From the chaos an army is formed – an army that's ready for war!

DATA

- **Skill:** 8
- **Speed:** 4
- **Strength:** 5
- **Intelligence:** 8
- **Powers:** summons sand army, staff shoots heat-rays

Drakona

Trained by a legendary kung fu master, Drakona is the most deadly ninja on the planet. The villain sees a flash of gold out of the corner of his eye... but it's already too late.

DATA

- **Skill:** 10
- **Speed:** 8
- **Strength:** 5
- **Intelligence:** 5
- **Powers:** expert martial artist, super agility and reflexes

Huracán

Carlos Cruz found a temple buried deep in the rainforest. Inside, he saw a strange medallion. Thunder rolled as he picked it up, sparks flew up his arm – and in a blinding flash he became Huracán, the maker of storms.

DATA

- Skill: 8
- Speed: 7
- Strength: 7
- Intelligence: 6
- Powers: creates storms, shoots lightning bolts from either hand

Glossary

- **AI program:** a computer program that simulates human intelligence

- **clone:** an exact copy

- **drone:** a machine that's controlled from a distance

- **hack:** break into a secure computer system

- **immortal:** can't die

- **impenetrable:** can't be broken through

- **kung fu:** Chinese martial arts

- **medallion:** a circular piece of metal, often very valuable and decorative

- **microbot:** a microscopic robot

- **ninja:** a secret agent who specialises in close combat and sabotage

- **penetrate:** to force a way into something

- **replication:** making a copy

- **sidekick:** an assistant

- **supercooled suit:** a suit containing an extremely cold liquid

- **supervillain:** a villain who's as powerful as a superhero

- **telescopic vision:** vision that can zoom in on distant objects

- **virus:** a type of germ

- **vortex:** a whirling mass of fluid or air, such as a whirlpool or tornado

Edited by Sam Taplin
With thanks to Chris Ball
Digital manipulation by Keith Furnival

First published in 2016 by Usborne Publishing Ltd, Usborne House, 83-85 Saffron Hill, London EC1N 8RT, England. www.usborne.com
Copyright © 2016 Usborne Publishing Ltd. The name Usborne and the devices 🖋 🎈 are Trade Marks of Usborne Publishing Ltd. All rights reserved.
No part of this publication may be reproduced, stored in a retrieval system or transmitted in any form or by any means, electronic, mechanical,
photocopying, recording or otherwise without the prior permission of the publisher. First published in America in 2016. UE. Printed in China.

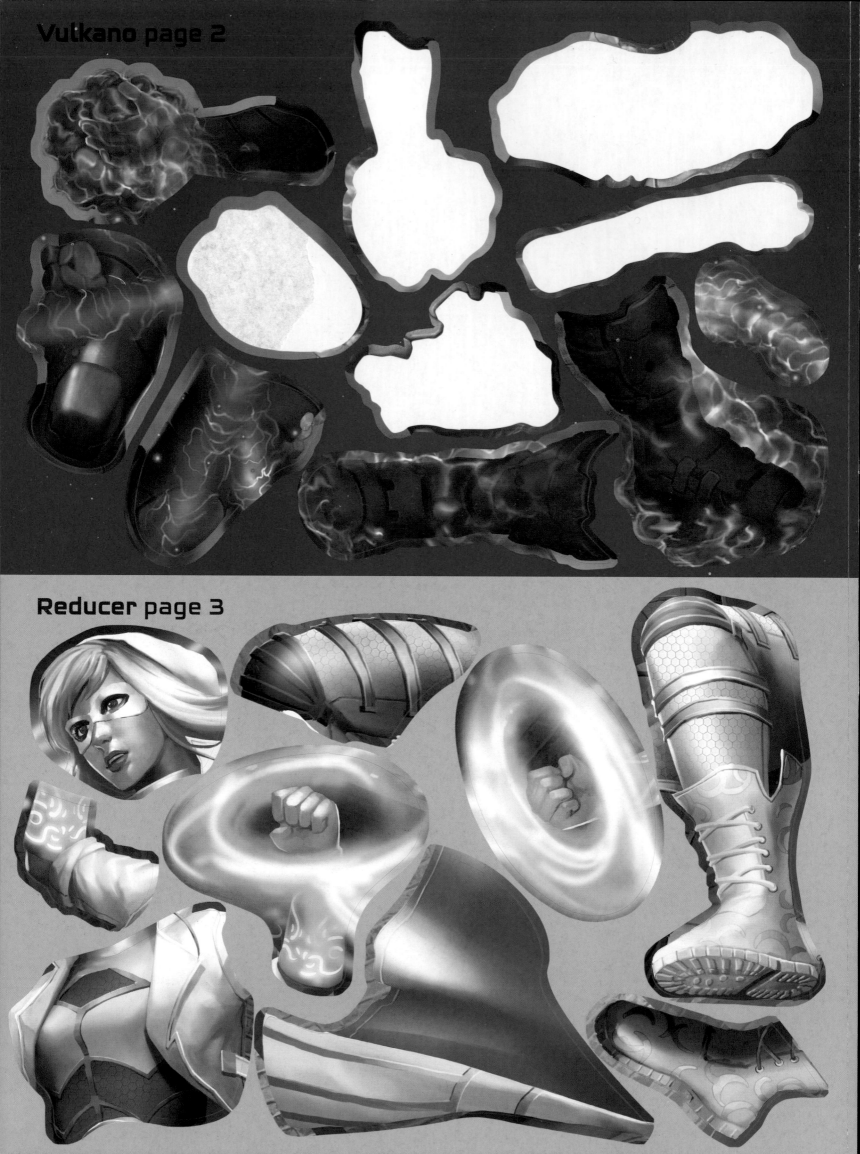

Vulkano page 2

Reducer page 3

Major Laser page 10

Xponential page 11

Coax page 12

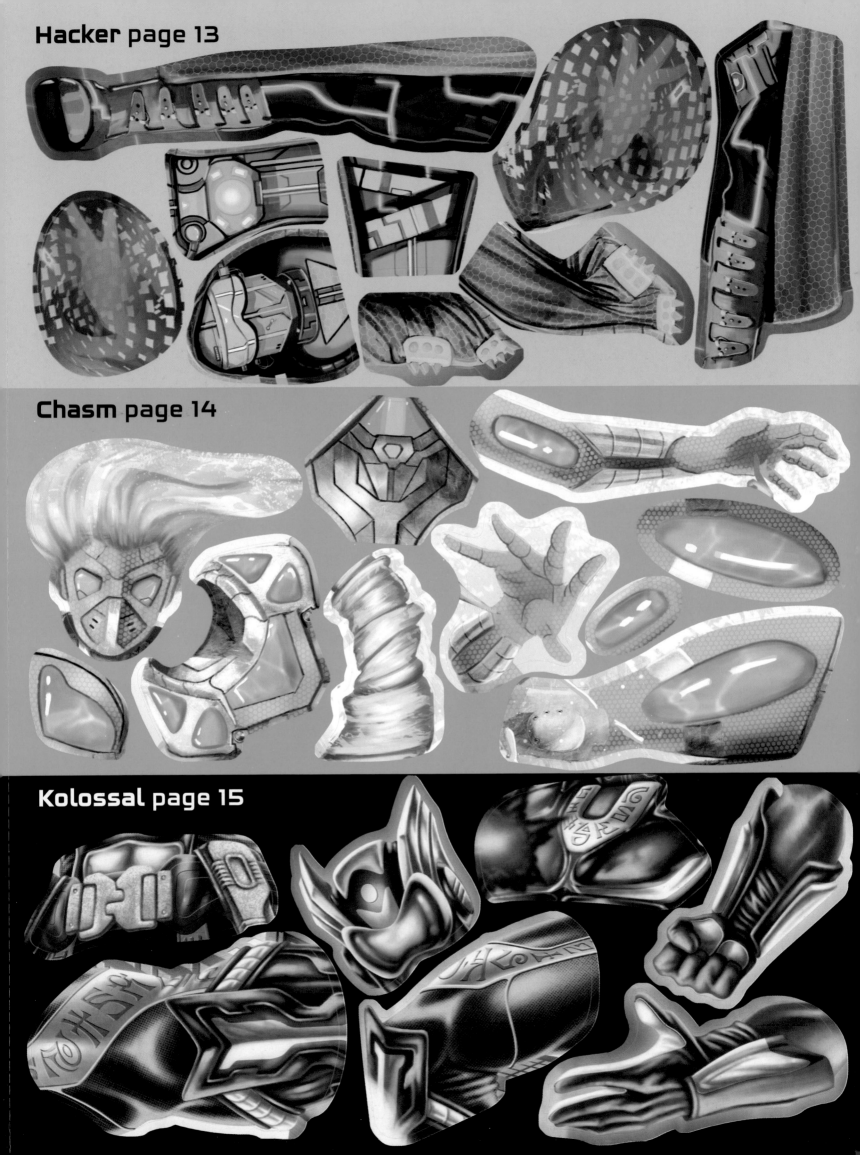

Hacker page 13

Chasm page 14

Kolossal page 15

Voide page 16

Leona page 17

Mason page 19

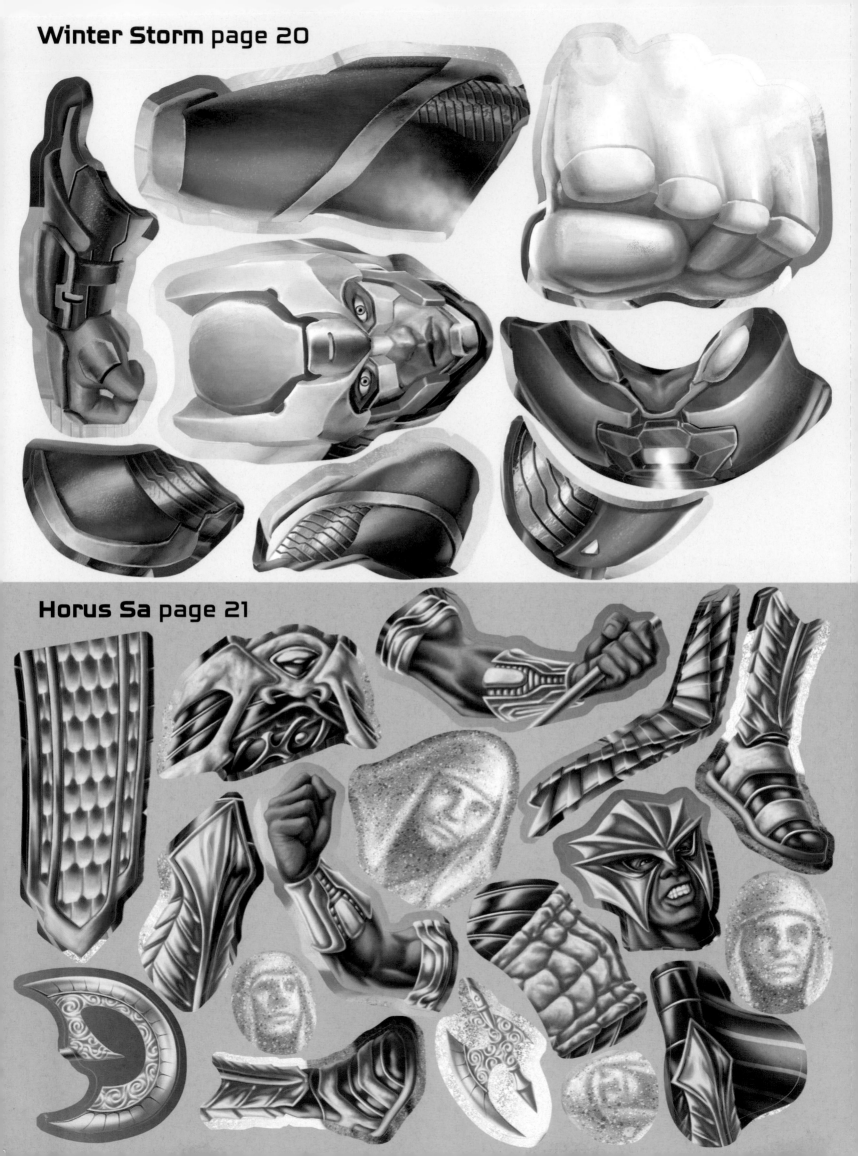

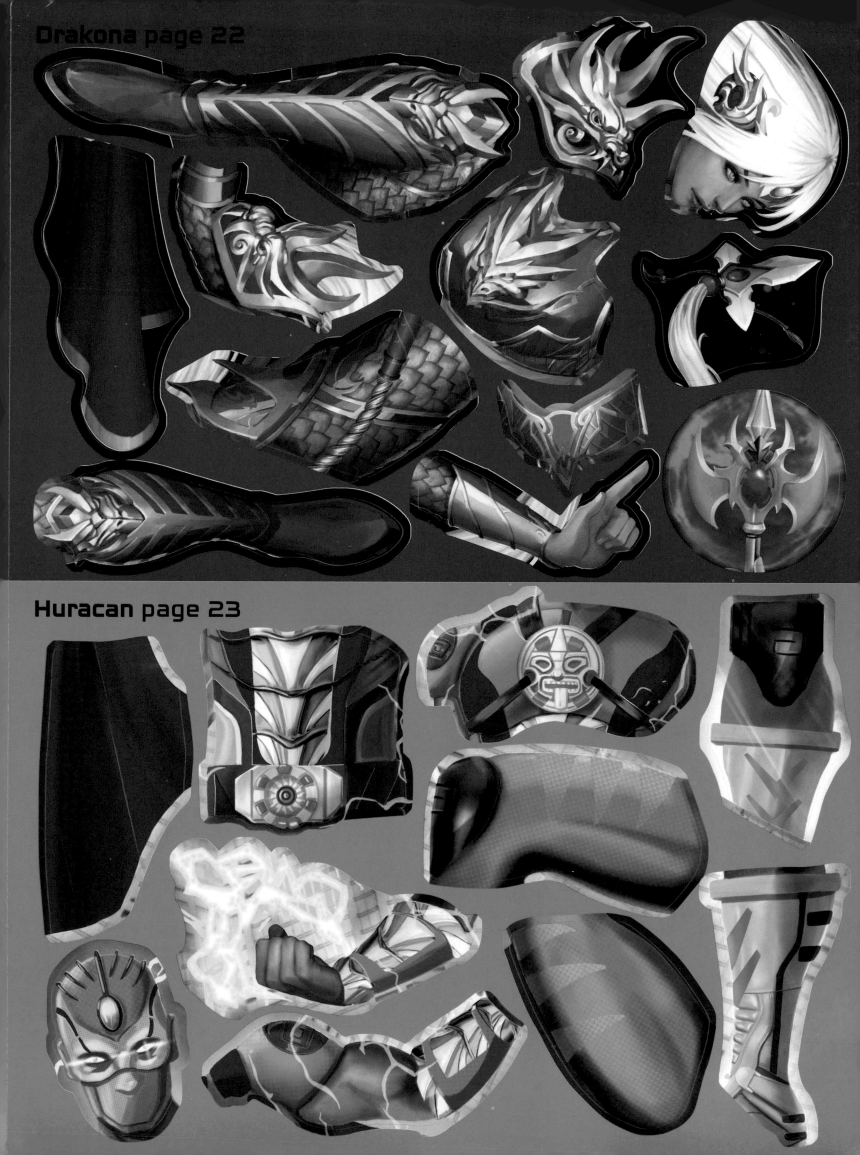